Anonymous

Japan and the Japanese

Written and Compiled from the Record of the American Expedition, and

the Best Sources

Anonymous

Japan and the Japanese
Written and Compiled from the Record of the American Expedition, and the Best Sources

ISBN/EAN: 9783337184490

Printed in Europe, USA, Canada, Australia, Japan

Cover: Foto ©Andreas Hilbeck / pixelio.de

More available books at **www.hansebooks.com**

INFORMATION FOR THE MILLION.

JAPAN

AND THE JAPANESE.

WRITTEN AND COMPILED FROM THE RECORD OF THE AMERICAN EXPEDITION, AND THE BEST SOURCES.

BY AN ORIENTAL TRAVELLER

NEW YORK:
FREDERIC A. BRADY, PUBLISHER,
24 ANN STREET.
1860.

JAPAN AND THE JAPANESE.

In history, the Japanese do not make such extravagant pretensions to antiquity as the Hindoos and Chinese. They are content with going back to the commencement of the reign of their first spiritual monarch, whose name was Sinmu, or at full length Sinmu Tenu, meaning "the supreme of all men," and the divine conqueror, a descendant of the gods. He was the first emperor, the supposed civilizer of the Japanese, and ascended the throne 660 years B.C. From his reign to A.D. 71 there reigned only ten emperors, which gives an average of seventy-three years to each reign! The first of the emperors is reported to have lived 167 years, and to have reigned ninety-eight. From A.D. 71 to 1690, there reigned 104 emperors, which makes the average duration of a reign in this period fifteen years and seven months, its shortness being, in a great measure, attributable to the very frequent practice of abdication, sometimes voluntary, and sometimes involuntary. We may notice a few of the most remarkable events of this long period. In 693 the art of making saki was discovered. In 749, gold, which had heretofore been imported from China, was first found in Japan. In 788, a strange people, not Chinese, invaded Japan, and their final expulsion involved a war of eighteen years. In 1147 was born Yozitorno, the first secular emperor. Placed in command of an army to suppress rebellion, this personage used the power thus intrusted to him for his own aggrandizement, by usurping nearly the whole temporal authority of his sovereign, leaving him little more than the spiritual, and thus establishing the form of government which has existed down to our time. In 1284 the Mogul Tartar conquerors of China invaded Japan with an armada of 4,000 ships, carrying a force, according to the Japanese, of 240,000 men. This was the celebrated expedition of Kublai Khan (grandson of the renowned Jenghis), the patron of Marco Polo. This great armada, like the Spanish against England, was nearly destroyed by a storm. Had it effected a landing in sufficient force, it is probable that it would have made a conquest of Japan, as the people who fitted it out had just made of China.

Japan was first made known to Europe by Marco Polo, who was in China at the time of the Mogul expedition. This, however, did not lead to its discovery. A Chinese junk, manned by Portuguese, was driven upon the coast by a storm, in 1542, fifty-four years after the arrival of the Portuguese in India. In 1549, seven years after the discovery, the Jesuits, headed by Francis Xavier, the famous apostle of the Indies, made their appearance in Japan, and forthwith the labor of converting the inhabitants went on prosperously until 1587, or for thirty-eight years, when it was partially arrested by the first persecution, which was of no great severity. This took place under Taico Sama, the most illustrious of all the secular emperors of Japan, a man who, by mere force of character, had, from the condition of a hewer of wood, raised himself to the throne. The native priesthood took alarm at the rapid spread of Christianity; and, in 1587, the emperor issued a proclamation prohibiting his subjects, under pain of death, from embracing the new religion; and several persons were executed for disobedience. It does not appear, however, that more than six or seven and twenty suffered on this occasion. . The son of Taico, himself a usurper, was dethroned by another usurper; and under him the persecution of Christianity became terrible, for, in 1590, it is stated that no fewer than 20,570 Christians were put to death. Another persecution followed in 1597, when, among others that suffered, were some European priests, that were crucified. After this a lull of forty years took place, when the persecution was renewed in 1637; and in a single day of the ensuing year, the 12th of April, 37,000 Christians were put to death. The persecution of the Roman emperors were trifles to such wholesale butcheries. During the two following years the Spaniards and Portuguese were finally expelled. The Romish priesthood boast that before the first persecution they had made 1,800,000 converts, and that in the year that followed it they made 12,000, so that in all they had probably converted not far from two millions of Japanese, reckoning among their proselytes several of the vassal princes.

The decree which isolated Japan from the rest of the world is as follows: "No Japanese ship or boat whatsoever, nor any native of Japan, shall presume to go out of the country. Whoso acts contrary to this shall die, and the ship, with the crew and goods aboard, shall be sequestrated till further orders. All Japanese who return from abroad shall be put to death. Whoever discovers a Christian priest shall have a reward of from 400 to 500 shuets (from $1,525 to $1,905), and for every Christian in proportion. All persons who propagate the doctrine of the Christians (the worship of the Fathers), or bear this scandalous name, shall be imprisoned in the Ombra, or common jail of the town. The whole race of the

Portuguese, with their mothers, nurses, and whatever belongs to them, shall be banished to Macao. Whoever presumes to bring a letter from abroad, or to return after he has been banished, shall die, with all his family; and whoever presumes to intercede for him shall be put to death. No nobleman, nor any soldier, shall be suffered to purchase anything of a foreigner."

The Japanese government acted fully up to the letter of its bloody decree of proscription. In 1640, three years after its publication, and the year which immediately followed the practical expulsion of the Portuguese and Spaniards, the Portuguese governor of Macao sent a mission to Japan, which, with its retinue, amounted to seventy-three persons. On their arrival at Nagaski, the whole were arrested, and an order came in due time from the emperor, directing them to be beheaded, and it was carried into effect on all but twelve of the meanest persons, reserved for the purpose of carrying back a threatening message, to the effect, that "Should the king of Portugal, nay, the very God of the Christians, presume to enter his dominions, he would serve them in the very same manner."

The ceremony of trampling on the cross was instituted on the expulsion of the Christians. It seems, however, always to have been confined to those parts in which the Christians had obtained their chief footing—namely, the town of Nagaski, and the provinces of Omura and Bungo, in the island of Kiu-siu. The proscription of one particular form of worship, when so many other religions or sects were tolerated, or viewed with indifference, is easily explained. The new religion was propagated by an energetic race of men, and its votaries inspired with an active zeal unknown to all the old forms of worship. Christianity, in a word, was proscribed, not on account of its tenets, but on account of the danger apprehended from those who taught it. The persecution was not a religious, but a political one. Its ministers and followers threatened the subversion of the native government and the institutions, and the substitution of a foreign yoke. They were deemed guilty of high treason, and punished according to the bloody code of Japan. According to Japanese notions, a dangerous insurrection was suppressed by the extermination of the insurgents. In this matter the Japanese acted with foresight; for there can be little doubt but that the Portuguese and Spaniards would in due course, and through the instrumentality of religion, have effected the conquest of Japan, unless we suppose them, which is highly improbable, to have acted with a forbearance which neither

Spanish, Dutch, nor English have exhibited in other parts of the East. The Japanese not only saw this, but very plainly expressed it. Thus, when the Spanish governor of the Philippines, in the year 1597, sent an envoy to the emperor to remonstrate with him respecting the persecution of the Christians, he addressed the Spanish official as follows: " Conceive yourselves in my position, the ruler of a great empire, and suppose certain of my subjects should find their way into your possessions, on the pretence of teaching the doctrine of Sinto. If you should discover their assumed zeal in the cause of religion to be a mere mask for ambitious projects—that their real object was to make themselves masters of your dominions, would you not treat them as traitors to the state? I hold the Fathers to be traitors to my state, and as such I treat them."

The priests of the various ancient forms of worship, a numerous body—for in the ecclesiastical capital alone they amounted to 52,169 with 6,020 temples—were equally interested with the government in the suppression of the rival, and to them, dangerous religion. The violence, insolence, and indiscretion of the Fathers, provoked the native priesthood beyond bearing. The Jesuits eulogize one of the converted tributary chiefs for his zeal, alleging that he had destroyed heathen temples. and monasteries, reckoned by some at no fewer than 3,000. Some of these tributary princes even went the length of sending an embassy to the pope, and king of Spain, which the emperor would not fail to consider an act of high treason. About the time that the first edict against Christians was published, the emperor dispatched two imperial commissioners to Father Cuello, demanding an answer and explanation to the following questions: "Why he and his associates forced their creed on the subjects of the emperor? Why they incited their disciples to destroy the national temples? Why they persecuted the Bonzes (priests)? Why they and the rest of their nation used for food animals useful to man, such as oxen and cows? And finally, why they permitted the merchants of their nation to traffic in his subjects, and carry them away as slaves to the Indies?" Evasive answers only were given to these demands, but the destruction of the temples and the traffic in slaves were not denied. With such provocations as these, we cannot wonder at persecution, although shocked at the ferocity and vindictiveness of the excesses. It is often affirmed, by people of great credit among the Japanese themselves, that pride and covetousness in the first place—pride amongst the great, and covetousness in the people of less note—contributed very much to the fall of the Portuguese by rendering them all odious. In our time the persecution, with the murder of ambassadors, would certainly be avenged by invasion, very probably ending in the conquest of Japan. Even in the seventeenth century Spain would probably have engaged in such an enterprise from the Philippines, had she not about this time been separated from Portugal; and the naval superiority of the Dutch, in alliance with the Japanese, proved an insuperable obstacle.

The Dutch made their first appearance in Japan in 1600, fifty-eight years after its discovery by the Portuguese, and about half a century after the latter nation had been carrying on trade with it. In common with the Portuguese, and eventually with the Spaniards, they carried on an active and profitable intercourse, down to the time of the exclusion of these two nations. The seat of commerce was at Firando, in the island of Kiu-siu. When the last persecution of Catholic Christianity was in progress, the Dutch furnished information of the political intrigues of their commercial rivals to the Japanese. They were called upon to assist in destroying the last refuge of the Japanese Christians in Simabarra, in Kiu-siu, and effected with the cannon of their ships what had baffled the skill of the imperial forces. This last event happened in 1639, and two years after, imperial commissioners arrived in Firando to remonstrate with them respecting what appeared to be very venial proceedings. They were addressed: "In former times, it was well known to us, that you both served Christ, but on account of the bitter enmity you ever bore each other, we imagined there were two Christs. Now, however, the emperor is assured to the contrary. Now, he knows you both serve one and the same Christ. From any indication of serving him you must in future forbear. Moreover, in certain buildings which you have newly erected, there is a date carved, which is reckoned from the birth of Christ. These buildings you must raze to the ground forthwith." The order was incontinently complied with; but their prompt obedience did not save the Dutch from being removed in 1641 from Firando and its comparative liberty to the virtual imprisonment on the island of Dezima in the harbor of Nagaski.

In 1613 we have the first authentic information of the English having attempted an intercourse with Japan; but it is certain, from the accurate information concerning the country, that they must have frequented it much earlier. William Adams, an Englishman, who acted as pilot to the first Dutch vessel that arrived at Japan, and had settled there, induced his countrymen to establish a trade. Accordingly, a ship called the Clove, commanded by Captain John

Sares, was dispatched for Japan, and reached Firando on the 11th June, 1613. Adams, who stood high in favor, obtained for his countrymen a most favorable reception, and, in a letter to the king of England, the emperor desires " the continuance of friendship with your highness—and that it may stand with your good liking to send your subjects to any part of our dominions, where they shall be most heartily welcome; applauding much their worthiness in the admirable knowledge of navigation, having with much facility discovered a country so remote, being no whit amazed with the distance of so mighty a gulf, nor greatness of such infinite clouds and storms, from prosecuting honorable enterprises of discoveries and merchandising—wherein they shall find me to further them according to their desires." The English, however, did not succeed, and after ten years' trial, in which they expended $200,000, they withdrew from the country. In 1653, a fruitless attempt was made to renew the British intercourse with Japan, said to have been defeated by the Dutch informing the Japanese that the queen of England was a daughter of the king of Portugal. The failure is not to be regretted, since it is certain that under the influence of a monopoly, such as that of the East India Company, trade could not have prospered in Japan, or anywhere else.

It is not necessary to advert to any of the subsequent small and futile attempts made to open an intercourse with long locked Japan, since they are all superseded by the more successful attempt recently made by the government of this country. To the United States of America belongs the credit of having been the first to reëstablish commercial relations with Japan. The increased traffic of that part of the world, particularly between eastern Asia and northwestern America, and the importance of the whale fishery in the Japanese seas, rendered it very desirable to have free access to at least some of the ports of Japan. Repeated attempts had been made by England, Russia, and the United States without success, when at length the United States government resolved to make an effort worthy of the object, and accordingly fitted out an expedition under Commodore M. C. Perry. The commodore sailed from Norfolk, in the Mississippi war-steamer, on the 24th of November, 1852, to be followed as soon as possible by the other vessels of the expedition. He arrived at the Bay of Yeddo on July 8th, 1853, with four vessels, two war-steamers and two sloops-of-war, and after some negotiations he delivered the letter of the President, promising to return for an answer in the spring. The rest of the year was spent at Loo Choo and China, and on the

12th of February, 1854, the squadron reappeared in the Bay of Yeddo, having by this time been increased to nine vessels, three steam frigates, four sloops-of-war, and two store ships. A treaty was concluded on the 31st of March, in terms of which the ports Simoda in the island of Nipon, and Hakodadi in Yesso, are opened for the reception of American ships, where they will be supplied with wood, water, provisions, coal, and other articles, so far as the Japanese possess them. Ships in distress, or from stress of weather, may enter other ports; and seamen shipwrecked on any part of the coast are to be aided and carried either to Simoda or Hakodadi. Seamen and others temporarily residing at these ports are, at Simoda, free to go anywhere within the limits of 17 miles from a small island in the harbor, and in like manner at Hakodadi within 12 miles. Ships of the United States are also permitted to trade under such regulations as shall be temporarily established by the Japanese government for the purpose. All the privileges that may hereafter be granted to any other nation, are to be accorded to the United States, and an embassy sent from the emperor of Japan to the President—which embassy, under one pretence or another, has been delayed for six years, and only now reached our shores.

About six months after the American treaty was

concluded, an English squadron, consisting of a frigate and three steamers, under the command of Rear Admiral Sir James Stirling, entered Nagaski. The primary object of this visit to Japan was to search for Russian vessels; but it was also intended to attempt to establish friendly relations between the two nations. A treaty was entered into, the effect of which is to open absolutely to British ships of every description, for effecting repairs, and obtaining fresh water, provisions and other supplies, two of the most convenient harbors in Japan—Nagaski and Hakodadi—to open inferentially to British ships in distress any other port in Japan it may be expedient for them to seek shelter in; to secure eventually to British ships and subjects in every port in Japan which may hereafter be open to foreigners, equal advantages with the ships, citizens, or subjects, of the most favored nation—excepting only the advantages at present accorded to the Dutch and Chinese. It imposes in return for these concessions no other obligation than that of respecting the laws and ordinances of the ports entered. The Russians and French have since succeeded in obtaining a similar footing in Japan.

The empire of Japan consists of a chain of islands lying off the eastern coast of Asia, and extending southeast and northwest between latitudes 31° and

48° and east longitude 129° and 150°. Inclosed between this chain and the opposite coasts of Corea and Manchu Tartary, is the Sea of Japan, which communicates by means of straits with the Chinese Sea on the south, the Pacific Ocean on the east, and the Sea of Okhotsk on the north.- To the east Japan has no nearer land than California, 5,000 miles off; the nearest port of China is 420 miles, and Kamtschatka 270 miles distant. The word Japan is probably a corruption of the Chinese name, Jih-pun-quo, that is, Kingdom of the Source of the Sun, or Eastern Kingdom. Marco Polo, who, as has been stated, was the first to bring intelligence of it to Europe, and who acquired his information in China, called it Zipanga. The Japanese name is Nipon, or Nifon—that is "Sun Source."

The empire is divided into Japan proper—consisting of the three large islands of Nipon, Kiu-siu, and Sitkokf. Nipon, the largest and more important of the group, and that which gives name to the whole empire, has an estimated era of 100,000 square miles; its length being more than 900 miles, while its average breadth exceeds 100. It is about one-fifth part larger than Great Britain. Its form is that of a curve or crescent, with the concave side toward the mainland. South of Nipon, and separated from it by a narrow channel, is the island of Kiu-siu, or

Ximo, about 200 miles in length and about 30 in average breadth, thus containing an area of about 16,000 square miles. Lying northeast of Kiu-siu, and eastward of the southern extremity of Nipon, is the island of Sitkokf, or Sikoko, about 150 miles in length by 70 in average breadth. It is separated from Nipon by a long strait, in some parts not more than a mile in width, and from Kiu-siu by Bungo Channel, which is about thirty miles broad. North of Nipon is the large island of Yesso, a conquest and colony of the empire. Its form is that of an irregular triangle, and its area is computed at 20,000 square miles. The southern portions of the island of Krafto, or Sagalien, which is separated from Yesso by the strait of Perouse, and the three southermost of the Kurile Islands belong to Japan.

The small islands that surround these are generally rocky and barren, but occasionally rich and fruitful. The entire number of islands composing the empire of Japan is estimated above 1,000, and the area of the whole at no less than 170,000 square miles. The coasts are difficult of access, not only from the multitude of rocks and islets which beset the passages, but also from the severe gales which agitate these narrow seas. Several dangerous whirlpools also occur among the rocks. It has been remarked that nature seems to have designed these islands to be a sort of little world, secluded and independent from the rest, as well by rendering it dangerous to approach their shores, as by endowing them plentifully with everything necessary for luxury and comfort, and thus enabling them to subsist without any commerce with other nations. The Japanese policy, which rigidly forbids all intercourse with strangers, in other circumstances impracticable, has been greatly facilitated by the interposition of these barriers.

The climate of Japan must vary considerably between its northern and southern extremities; but except at a few points, we possess very little information on the subject. At Nagaska, in the island of Kiu-siu, latitude 33°, the average temperature in the month of January was 35°, and in August 98° of Fahrenheit. At this place the weather is very changeable. Rain is frequent at all seasons of the year, but especially in the months of July and August. In December and January the ground is covered with hoar frost, and occasionally with snow except in mild winters. In summer the land is cooled by the sea breeze which blows from the south during the day and from the east at night. At Simoda, on the island of Nipon, in latitude 34° 39′, we learn from the account of the American expedition that the climate was more or less variable in the winter and spring.

The presence of snow upon the lofty peaks, although there is seldom frost or snow at Simoda itself, and not unfrequent rains and fogs, give an occasional humidity and rareness to the atmosphere, which is chilly to the senses, and must be productive of inflammatory diseases, such as are frequent in spring and winter with us. The change of wind alternates often between the warm sea-breezes from the south, and the cold blasts from the snow-capped mountains inland, and produces the usual effects of such variations. In summer it is occasionally very hot in the daytime, but the nights are refreshed with cool breezes. From April 19 to May 13, a record of the thermometer gives 72° as the highest, and 58° as the lowest point; and of the barometer 29° 38', and 30°. A Russian officer, who was for two years a prisoner at Hakodadi, in Yesso, latitude 41° 49', says that the lakes freeze, snow lies in the valleys and plains from November to April, and falls in as great abundance as at St. Petersburg. Severe frosts are uncommon, yet the temperature is often two degrees below the freezing point. In summer, the rain pours in torrents at least twice a week, the horizon is obscured by dark clouds, violent winds blow, and the fog is scarcely ever dispersed. Apples, pears, and peaches hardly attain ripeness, and the orange and lemon will not bear fruit. Of the climate of the still more northern part of the empire we have no precise account; but the same authority informs us, that on the coast of Sagalien, which is but little further north than Paris, the sea is not clear of ice so early as the Gulf of Finland. Fogs are very prevalent in Japan, and thunder storms are frequent.

The surface of the principal islands is in general very irregular, though in the interior some plains of very considerable extent occur. In many places hills descend close to the seashore, or leave only a narrow strip of land between the water and their bases. The highest mountain is said to be Fuzi, an extinct volcano, on the island of Nipon, westward of the bay of Yeddo. Its summit is clad in perpetual snow, thus indicating a height of not less than 12,000 feet above the level of the sea. Several mountains of considerable elevation are seen to rise in the northern part of Nipon, in Yesso, and in Sagalien, and some of them are active volcanoes. Besides the outburst of frequent volcanic eruptions, no country is more frequently visited by destructive earthquakes. Earthquakes are said to be so frequent that the natives regard them no more than we do ordinary storms. In 1586 a succession of earthquakes took place, and lasted forty days, causing the destruction of the best part of the city of Yeddo, and the death, it is alleged, of 200,000 of its inhabitants. Many volcanic eruptions and severe earthquakes are recorded as having taken place between that time and the present. In December, 1854, an earthquake which occurred, was felt on the whole coast. Of the town of Simoda only a few temples and private edifices, that stood on elevated spots, escaped destruction. The fine city of Osaca, on the southeastern side of Nipon, was completely destroyed, and the capital of Yeddo did not escape without injury. On the 10th of November, 1855, an earthquake at Yeddo is said to have caused the destruction of 100,000 dwellings, and 54 temples, and the death of 30,000 persons.

The rivers are numerous, but short, shallow, and rapid. They are not navigable for vessels of burden, but some of them may be ascended, by small boats, for some miles from the sea. The principal lake in Japan, is that of Oitz, in the southern part of Nipon. It is about 60 miles in length, but of inconsiderable breadth.

Little is at present known of the geological formation of the Japanese islands. The volcanic formation appears to prevail, but by no means to the exclusion of the sedimentary. The usual mineral products, as far as yet known, are gold, silver, copper, quicksilver, tin, lead, iron, coal, sulphur and salt. With the exception of tin and iron, these seem to be very abundant. The gold is found in many parts of the empire, sometimes as ore, and sometimes from the washings of the earth and sand. Silver is equally plentiful with gold, and it is probable that the quantity of these metals annually exported from the country, when the trade was open, amounted to $7,000,000, or $8,000,000. Copper abounds throughout the whole group, and sometimes of a quality not to be surpassed by any in the world. The natives refine it, and cast it into cylinders about a foot long and an inch thick. Iron ore, rich enough for the purpose of smelting, appears to be confined to three provinces, and the metal is consequently very dear. Lead and quicksilver are said to be abundant, but they have never been an article of export. Tin has been discovered in small quantities, and of a quality so fine and white that it almost equals silver; but of the extent to which it may be procured, little is known, as the Japanese do not attach much value to it. Sulphur is so abundant, that in many places it lies in broad, deep beds, and may be dug up and removed with as much ease as sand. Coal is found in many parts of the country; the mines are skillfully worked, and it is used for fuel by the people. No diamonds have been found; but agates, carnelians, and jaspers are met with, some of them of great beauty. Pearls, often of great size and beauty, are fished up on nearly all parts of the coast.

The vegetable productions of Japan are, for the most part, those common to temperate regions. Timber is, however, so scarce that no one is permitted to cut down a tree without permission from the magistrate, and only on condition of planting a young one in its stead. The most common forest trees are the fir and cedar, the latter growing to an immense size, being sometimes more than eighteen feet in diameter. Two species of oak are found in the northern part of the empire. The mulberry grows wild, in great abundance. In the south the bamboo cane, though a tropical plant, is found, and largely used in manufactures of various sorts. The camphor-tree is very valuable, and lives to a great age. The camphor is made from a decoction of the roots and stems, cut in small pieces. Chestnut and walnut-trees are both found. Among the fruit-trees, are the orange, lemon, fig, plum, cherry and apricot.

Extensive cultivation leaves no room for wild animals, and the tame animals not being used for food, are not multiplied beyond the necessity for their use. The horses are small, but hardy, durable and active. William Adams, an English mariner, already mentioned, of the time of King James I., describes them as "not tall, but of the size of our middling nags, short and well trust, small headed and very full of metal, in my opinion far exceeding the Spanish jennet in pride and stomach." Oxen and cows are only used in ploughing and carriage, milk and butter not being articles of food. Buffaloes of an extraordinary size, with hunches on their backs, like camels, are used to draw carts, and carry heavy goods on their backs. Swine are a great item of trade with the Chinese. Dogs are to be found in large numbers, in the half domesticated state in which they generally exist in the East. This is not true, however, of one species resembling a King Charles spaniel, which is considered very valuable. It is conjectured that the variety known to us may have sprung from some presented by the emperor to the king of England. The wild animals are bears, boars, foxes, monkeys, deer and hares. Rats and mice are very common, as well as two small species of weasel, or ichneumon, which live, half tame, under the eaves of houses.

Wild fowl are very abundant, consisting chiefly of geese and ducks, which migrate in great numbers to the shores of Japan, in winter. Numerous species of pigeons are to be found, and woodcocks, pheasants, snipes, larks, etc., are common. There are two species of pheasant, and one of peacock, peculiar to Japan. Domestic poultry are kept by the natives almost solely for ornament or amusement. Some of the reptilia are of large size, and along with the insect tribes, are dreaded for their deadly and destructive powers.

The Japanese are an active, vigorous people, of the middle size, and in their bodily and mental powers, more closely assimilated to Europeans than Asiatics. The common people are of a yellow color, which sometimes borders on brown, and sometimes on white. The classes which expose the upper parts of their bodies in summer, have their naturally fair complexion deepened into brown. Their dark brown eyes are oblong, small, and sunk deep in their head. The eyelids forming a deep furrow, gives them the appearance of being keen-sighted. Their heads are large, and their necks short, their hair black and glossy with oil. Their noses, without being flat, are yet rather thick and short. The ladies of distinction, who seldom go out in the open air without being covered, are perfectly white, and the cheeks of the young display a blooming carnation color. The married women of Japan dye the teeth black, by means of a corrosive composition, so powerful that by mere touch it burns the flesh into a purple, gangrenous spot, and in spite of the utmost care in the application, invariably taints the gums, destroying their ruddy color and vitality. With the exception of the black teeth, of those who are married, the Japanese women are not ill-looking. The young girls are well formed, and rather pretty.

In the ordinary mutual intercourse of friends and families, the women have their share, and rounds of visiting and tea-parties are kept up as briskly in Japan as in the United States. Superficial observation led to the belief that Japan was colonized by the Chinese; but a more accurate knowledge of the physical characteristics and language of the people, has rendered this opinion untenable. Indeed, the Japanese themselves consider it a great disgrace to be compared with the Chinese. The structure of the languages of the two countries is essentially different; that of Japan being polysyllabic, while all the dialects of the Chinese are monosyllabic. It is true that, like the Latin in Europe during the middle ages, the Mandarin dialect of the Chinese is in use among the learned in Japan, as in Corea, Yonquin, and elsewhere: and hence many Chinese words have found their way into the Japanese language; but the introduction of these only makes the structural difference the more apparent. The Yomi, or primitive language of Japan, is used in poetry and works of light literature. The Chinese language, slightly varied in pronunciation, is employed by the Bonzes, or priests, in their religious books. The vulgar language of the country is a mixture of the two. Close affinities have not been traced between the Yomi of Japan and other Asiatic languages. By some it is thought to be most like the language of the Tartar race, to which, in spite of diversity in physical characteristics, it is now most commonly believed that the Japanese belong. In regard to the population of Japan, all our information rests merely on conjecture. Some travellers have estimated it at 10,000,000, while others make it more than four or five times that amount. All, however, who have visited the country bear testimony to the populousness of the parts seen by them. Taking the average of the population of divisions of India—countries which, in nearly the same latitudes, when taken together, combine the principal features of the Japanese territory—we obtain 225 persons to the square mile as an exceedingly probable basis for calculating the population of Japan. This, in round numbers, would give the population of the four principal Japanese islands as 39,900,000. Taking the average all over China, according to the last census, as the basis of calculation, which gives 268 to the square mile, we would have a Japanese population of 42,000,000. The checks to this exuberant population are infanticide, which though prohibited by law is openly practised; and public prostitution, which is legalized. Pestilences, and occasional famines have periodically thinned a country wholly dependent on its own resources.

The Japanese are divided into classes, which are

all hereditary: a state of society that has a close resemblance to that of the Hindoos, while it differs widely from that of the Chinese. These classes, exclusive of the imperial families, are: 1st, The hereditary vassal princes of the empire; 2d, The hereditary nobility, who hold the lands as fiefs subject to military service to some one of the hereditary princes; 3d, The priests; 4th, The military, or soldiers of the nobility; 5th, The professional classes, including inferior officials, medical practitioners, and the like; 6th, The mercantile class, comprising all merchants and traders; 7th, The artisan class, including all crafts; and 8th, Unskilled laborers, including peasants, fishermen, and sailors. To this last class belongs the great mass of the people, who are, in fact, in a condition of villenage, and in so far as they are rural laborers, mere occupants. To these may be added a Pariah class, consisting of all persons dealing in leather, skins, and peltry, and who, from their constant contact with dead animal matter, are deemed in a state of perpetual pollution. They are not permitted to dwell among the rest of the people, and must live in villages by themselves. They dare not even enter an inn, tea-house, or any place of public entertainment; and no Japanese, not of their own class, would even touch or use a vessel out of which they had taken food. From them are taken the jailers and executioners. The first four classes have the privilege of wearing two swords, the fifth of wearing one, and all the five of wearing a particular kind of trowsers forbidden to the rest. Although the ranks of each are closed against the others, it does not appear that the line of class separation is always impassable. The most illustrious of all the secular emperors who reigned toward the end of the sixteenth century, rose to the throne from being a hewer and carrier of wood, from the mere force of superior endowment.

The form of government in Japan resembles, in no small degree, the feudal system of medieval Europe. The sovereign power is lodged in a supreme ruler, but the greater part of the country is subject to vassal princes, who pay tribute or render military service to the lord paramount. Not only every institution but nearly every office is hereditary, descending from father to son. According to Japanese history, a single race of sovereigns, reputed to be descended from the gods, governed the empire for 1800 years to A.D. 1195, when the then commander of the army while engaged in suppressing a rebellion, usurped the greater part of the secular power, leaving to the lawful sovereign little more than the spiritual. Hence rose the singular government which still exists, consisting of two sovereigns, the one invested with the whole secular power, the other only with the ecclesiastical. Both princes have separate courts or capitals, the spiritual chief residing in Miako, the temporal in Yeddo. The former, though nominally supreme, has not a particle of temporal power, being literally, from birth to death, shut up at Miako, in his little principality of Kioto, with the revenues of which, and the presents sent him by the temporal ruler, called the Siogun, or Ticoon, or Kubo Sama, he must be content. Even the government of his own principality is in the hands of some grandee of his court, so that there never lived a sovereign having less of the attributes of sovereignty. He is visited with great pomp once in seven years by the Siogun. Whatever may have at one time been the power of the Siogun or Ticoon, it is certain that it is now very much circumscribed; indeed, he is as much subject to laws as the meanest of his subjects. The real power of the empire is chiefly vested in the grand council of thirteen members, five belonging to the first class of society, the hereditary vassal princes, and the remaining eight to the second class, the nobility below the rank of princes. The chief or president of this council has the title of "Governor of the Empire," and in him is vested the supreme power. He decides upon all affairs of moment, appoints the various officers, and receives returns from all the authorities of the offices. His office appears to be hereditary. The grand council has even the power of dethroning the emperor. Important resolutions of the council are always laid before him, and he generally assents without investigation or delay; but should he not at once grant his assent, or disapprove of a measure, it is immediately referred to the arbitration of the three princes of the royal blood most nearly related to the Siogun, and their decision is final. If they differ in opinion from the monarch he must instantly relinquish the throne to his son, or some other heir, without even the power to retract. If, on the contrary, they agree with him, the member of council who proposed the rejected measure must die, and not unfrequently all who supported him. It has thus sometimes happened that the whole council, with the governor of the empire at their head, have been obliged by suicide to atone for a mistake in national policy. The vassal prince still exercises a kind of sovereign power within his own territories. Formerly the kingdom was sub-divided into sixty-six or sixty-eight principalities, which had previously formed independent kingdoms, and continued as principalities under the rule of their respective princes, subject however to forfeiture in the case of rebellion or treason. This penalty of forfeiture having been incurred by many of the reigning princes, advantage was taken of the circumstance to split the forfeited principalities into fragments, so that, instead of the original number, there are now no less than six hundred and four distinct administrations, including principalities, lordships, imperial provinces, and imperial towns, of which last the Siogun himself is the ruling lord. The chief danger to the empire lies in these princes, and accordingly strange and harassing means are employed to restrain their power. Their families are kept at court as hostages, and they themselves are obliged to pass half the year on every alternate year there, while they are kept poor by the large contingent of troops which they are compelled to furnish. They are allowed to exercise scarcely any function of administration, that is not merely ceremonial, the real administration being conducted by deputies appointed by the imperial council, two for each province. To secure the fidelity even of these, their families must constantly reside at Yeddo, the capital, while they themselves reside alternately at the capital and in the provinces. Besides these the princes are continually surrounded by numerous private spies, who, unknown to them, watch their domestic as well as public proceedings. In fact, the emperors, the governor of the empire, grand counsellors, vassal princes, down even to the humblest citizens, are all under the eye of a secret police. Every city or town is divided into groups of five families, and every member is held personally responsible for the conduct of the whole. Everything, therefore, that occurs in one of these families, out of the usual course, is instantly reported to the authorities by the other four to save themselves from censure. Such are the means by which an extensive but essentially feeble empire is held together, and hence arises the unalterable nature of the laws and customs. A governor, a lord, a prince, knows that if he attempts any alterations whatever, he will be instantly denounced by his colleague or secretary as a violator of the established usages of the empire, and the punishment of this crime is death. The same fear of the same inevitable doom deters the common people from making the slightest degree of change.

Thus a people naturally frank, and possessed of a high sense of honor, have become in public life cunning, treacherous and mean. The men of all classes are said to be exceedingly courteous, and although inquisitive about strangers, never becoming offensively intrusive. The rigid exclusiveness in regard to foreigners is a law merely enacted by the government from motives of policy, and not a sentiment of the Japanese people. Their habits are social among themselves. They have the character, from all travellers, of being very industrious, and persevering. They are satisfied with little, and live principally on vegetables, rice and fish. Water is their common drink. Although essentially an abstemious people, they are not averse, occasionally, to strong potations. The lower orders frequently drink to excess on holidays, but the sin of drunkenness is far less common than among ourselves.

Woman is recognized as a companion, and not treated as a slave. Her position is certainly not so elevated as among Christian nations, but the fact of the non-existence of polygamy is a distinctive feature which preëminently characterizes the Japanese as the most moral and refined of all the Eastern people. Concubinage, however, is common; and prostitution prevails to a very great extent. Public bagnios are licensed, and open from sunset to sunrise; their keepers rank with merchants, and are entitled to wear one sword and the distinguishing trowsers. One of the temples of Venus, at Yeddo, is as magnificent as a prince's palace, and contains 600 priestesses. It would appear, however, that there is something like moral revenge on the keepers of these establishments after death, for when they die, a bridle of straw is put in their mouths, and their bodies dragged through the streets to a dunghill, where they are left to be devoured by dogs. Captain Saris gave this very same account 200 years ago. The women of the lower order are frequently seen engaged in field labor, and employments which in other countries are considered to belong specially to the stronger sex, showing the general industry, and necessity of keeping every hand employed in this populous empire. All along the coast, says old Adams, "we found women divers that lived with their household and families in boats. These women would catch fish by diving, which the net and lines had missed, and that in eight fathoms deep."

The Japanese are distinguished by their neat, clean and orderly habits. They are very particular in keeping themselves, their clothes and houses clean and neat. The bath is in frequent use, their inns and houses being furnished with cold, hot and vapor baths. Their highways are good, and swept with a degree of regularity and nicety which it would be well for our city authorities to imitate. The distances are marked by posts, and, where practicable, the rivers crossed by bridges. Along the roads are numerous inns for the accommodation of travellers. Adams, on one occasion, accompanied the prince of Firando to the capital, who had with him a train of 3,000 persons, and he thus describes the hospitality of the march: "Such good order was taken for the passing and providing for these 3,000 soldiers, that no man either travelling or inhabiting upon the way where they lodged was any way injured by them, but chiefly entertained them as their guests, because they paid for what they took as all other men did. Every town and village upon the way being well fitted with cooks and victualling houses, where they might at an instant have what they needed, and diet themselves from a penny English a meal to two shillings a meal."

The Japanese at one time enjoyed a high reputation among Eastern nations for courage and military prowess. This, however, is no longer the case; and we suspect they will be found an essentially feeble and pusillanimous people. They are said to be deficient in courage, and in the art of war mere children. This can scarcely fail to be the case with a people who, by all accounts, have enjoyed peace external and internal for more than two centuries. A courageous and patient endurance of pain and suffering, and even a contempt for death, we know to be quite consistent with a lack of active aggressive courage.

Of the Japanese army little is known, except that it is very numerous, and that the military, like other classes, are hereditary. The officers and commanders, however, do not belong to the military order, but are princes and nobles, from which we may infer that the spirit and discipline of the Japanese army are not of a very high order. It consists of two classes, the soldiers of the emperor, and those of the vassal princes, the former being considered the better organized. Both consist of infantry and cavalry, armed with swords, lances, and bow and arrow, and occasionally with a matchlock.

The Japanese laws are very short and intelligible, and the proceedings under them are as simple as the laws themselves. There are no professional lawyers, every man being deemed competent to plead his own case. If a person is aggrieved, he appeals to the magistrate, who summons the other person before him. The case is then stated by the complainant in his own way, and the accused is heard in reply. The magistrate examines witnesses, and is said frequently to display great acuteness in the detection of falsehood. He passes sentence, from which there is no appeal, and it is carried into execution instanter. If the matter in dispute be of great importance, the magistrate may refer it to the emperor in council. Sometimes, in trifling cases, he orders the parties to go and settle the matter privately with the aid of friends, and it is well understood that it must be settled, or unpleasant consequences will result.

There is no country, not even excepting China, in which human life seems to be less valued than in Japan, whether by the government or the people themselves. Capital punishments extend even to the slightest offences, and suicide is not only frequent, but is considered meritorious. Disembowelling is the usual manner of committing suicide, and is performed by making two incisions in the form of a cross over the abdomen, while a trusty follower stands behind to complete the work by decapitation. Public executions are usually performed by beheading; crucifixion is also a mode in use. After execution, the bystanders amuse themselves by trying their own skill and the temper of their swords upon the corpse.

The great source of revenue in Japan is the rent of land, with an impost on houses, in the manner of a ground rent. There appears to be no tax on articles of consumption, no capitation tax, and no transit duties. The cultivators of the soil appear to be mere villeins. On lands belonging to the crown, the proportion of the crop considered rent is four parts in ten, and on the rest, six in ten, most commonly the latter. These proportions apply to every kind of crop—corn, pulses, and cotton. In order to determine the rent, the land is surveyed by sworn appraisers twice a year, once before the seed is sown, and again immediately after harvest. Those who cultivate untilled ground, have the crop for two or three years. Among their many excellent laws relating to agriculture, one is, that whosoever does not cultivate his ground for the term of one year, forfeits his possession. It would appear from the proportion of crop taken as rent, that the impost on the land does not materially differ from that assumed as land-tax under the Mohammedan government of Hindostan, and continued, in most parts of that country, by the British. This will enable us to make an approximate estimate of the rental of Japan—that is, of the principal source of its public income. This, of course, will suppose a similar condition of society and rate of population in Japan and the country with which it is compared. Let us take, therefore, the same Indian territories by which we have attempted to estimate the population. These districts have, in round numbers, a population of 46,000,000, and yield a land-tax of $50,000,000. This proportion would give Japan, with its estimated population of 40,000,000, a rental of $43,500,000 to be divided between the imperial government, feudatory princes, hereditary nobles, and soldiery. To the rent of land is to be added the ground rent of the houses, which is said to be at the rate of forty cents for each fathom of frontage, without regard to depth, unless it exceed fifteen fathoms, when the rate is doubled. Estimating the houses in the towns to contain an average of five inhabitants each, and also five fathoms of frontage, would give the income from this source at more than $16,500,000; or, adding this to the land-rent, would make the annual revenue of the empire about $60,000,000.

The Japanese being chiefly dependent on the soil for subsistence, have arrived at a high state of perfection in the art of agriculture. Though the greater part of the country is hilly or mountainous, and the soil in general rather poor, yet almost every available foot of land is cultivated, and very abundant crops are raised. Where the land is inaccessible to the plough it is cultivated by manual labor. Like the Chinese, they pay great attention to manuring and irrigation. As animal food constitutes hardly any part of their subsistence, no pastures or meadows are to be seen. Rice constitutes the main object of agriculture, as it forms the bread corn of the people from one end of the empire to the other. Its cultivation extends to the island of Yesso, and as far as forty-five degrees of north latitude. The rice of Japan is known to excel every other of Asia. From it the inhabitants distill a drink, in very great use among them, called "saki." Wheat and barley are grown, but the former is not much used, and the latter chiefly as provender for cattle. Rye, maize, and millet are also raised. Beans and peas of different kinds are cultivated in great abundance: particularly the bean from which soy, a kind of sauce, prepared by boiling and fermentation, is made. Among esculent roots and pot-herbs the following are successfully cultivated: the batata, potato, carrot, turnip, cabbage, radish, lettuce, gourd, melon, and cucumber. The fruits are much the same as those of this country.

The tea plant in Japan, as in China, takes the place of the vine in the temperate regions of the west, and of the coffee of tropical countries. The tea shrub is a very useful plant in Japan, and yet it is allowed no other room but round the borders of rice and corn fields, and in barren places unfit for the cultivation of other things. In consequence of this want of care, its leaves are unfit for the consumption of strangers. Its use, however, is universal among the natives. It was introduced into Japan, from China, in the ninth century. Tobacco was first introduced, by the Portuguese, in the early part of the sixteenth century, about the same time that it was taken to England, and it is remarkable that the Japanese emperor instituted a persecution against its growers and smokers at the same time that king James, the "British Solomon," issued his "Counter Blast," and with as little effect in arresting its use. The plants cultivated in Japan for textile purposes are cotton and hemp. The mulberry is grown for the silk-worm. In husbandry cotton ranks next in importance to rice, and furnishes material for clothing the great mass of the people.

In the manufacture of cotton fabrics the Japanese

display considerable skill, but in this respect they do not equal the Hindoos. Their best silk is equal to that of the Chinese. In the manufacture of porcelain they are said to excel the Chinese. Like the Chinese, the Japanese have long practised the manufacture of paper and glass. Formerly they did not know how to make the flat pane for window glass, and what they now make is of an inferior quality, as they still purchase thick mirror glass to grind into lenses. They manufacture paper in great abundance, as well for writing and printing, as for tapestry, handkerchiefs, etc. It is made of very various qualities, and some of it is as soft and flexible as cotton cloth. Indeed, that used for handkerchiefs might be mistaken for cloth, so far as toughness and flexibility are concerned. This paper is made from the bark of the mulberry by means of a peculiar process. The well known lacquer ware to which Japan has given a name, is unequalled for beauty and durability by that of any other nation. They display considerable skill in working metals. In wood-work, caskets, cabinets, and the like, they are unsurpassed. Some of their swords are equal to the finest Damascus blades; and their carpenters' and cabinetmakers' tools are as good in temper as those of a similar kind in this country. They are exceedingly quick in observing any improvement brought in among them by foreigners, and copy it with great skill and exactness. Clocks, watches, and astronomical instruments are made by them, copied from imported models.

In certain branches of the fine arts the Japanese have attained no small skill. They are ignorant, however, of anatomy and perspective, and therefore barbarous in their sculptures and landscapes; but in the representation of a single object, they manifest great accuracy of detail, and a truthful adherence to nature. Architecture, as an art, can hardly be said to have an existence—their temples, palaces, and private houses being all low and temporary structures, generally of wood; and the frequency of earthquakes leads them to bestow less care on their buildings than in other circumstances they might do.

The medical knowledge of the Japanese must necessarily be very imperfect, as their dread of pollution from contact with dead bodies prevents them from scientifically investigating the dead subject. The native physicians display great eagerness to acquire information on professional points from strangers; and Dr. Siebold speaks with high praise of the zeal with which they thronged around him from all parts of the empire, seeking to enlarge their stores of knowledge. He also bears testimony to their intelligence, as evinced by the questions they asked. Original medical works are constantly appearing, as well as translations of such Dutch medical books as they can best understand. Their drugs are mostly animal and vegetable; they are too little acquainted with chemistry to venture upon mineral remedies. They study medical botany with great attention, and display considerable knowledge of the virtues of plants. In the science of astronomy they are tolerably proficient. They understand the use of our instruments, and many of them are successfully imitated by native workmen. They calculate eclipses accurately; and yearly almanacs are prepared in the Yeddo and Dairi colleges. Their year consists of twelve lunar months, but is converted into sidereal time by the introduction, every third year, of an intercalary month of the requisite length. The natural day of twenty-four hours is divided into twelve watches—six for the day from sunrise to sunset, and six for the night from sunset to sunrise. As this division is absolute, it follows that the watches are never of the same length, except at the equinoxes. Their length is regulated only four times in the year, the intervening watches being consequently left in uncertainty. The twelve watches go by the names of the signs of the zodiac. These signs are the same as ours, differing only in their names. The chronology of the Japanese, like that of the Chinese, is usually reckoned by the reigns of their monarchs, beginning with the first supposed founder of the empire, who commenced his reign B.C. 660. They have also a cycle of sixty years, formed by multiplying the signs of the zodiac by the number of elements, which they, as the Hindoos, reckon to be five.

There are three religions, and numerous religious sects in Japan. The ancient religion of the country is called Sinsyu, that is, the gods' worship, and its followers are called Sintoos. In this worship the chief deity is the sun-goddess, Ten-sio-dai-zin. She is considered to be too exalted to be herself addressed in prayer. She is said to be invoked through inferior or subaltern deities called Kami, of whom there are said to be reckoned 492. Other religions of Asia have been so grossly misrepresented in the West by travellers either too ignorant, or too bigoted, to inquire into and report fairly upon their tenets, that we must be exceedingly careful in giving credence to the assertion that the Japanese worship such a multiplicity of gods. Upon inquiry and reflection, it will be found that, however the forms and external ceremonies may differ, common sense upon matters of religion is pretty equally divided among mankind: and we are more than inclined to think that the 492 inferior divinities of Japan are merely separate attributes of God. There are 2,640 deified men in their calendar, who, together with the 492 inferior gods, make a total of 3,132 divinities, who have each their temples, priests, and priestesses; the last being the wives of the priests, for celibacy forms no part of their worship. The more immediate end which the followers of the Sintoo faith are said to pursue is happiness in this world. The temples are generally in a grove of trees, or on the side of a green hill, and have avenues of cypresses leading to them, the buildings themselves being small and mean. The five great duties enjoined in the Sintoo religion are— 1st, Preservation of pure fire as an emblem of purity and an instrument of purification; 2d, Purity of soul and body, the former by obeying the dictates of reason and the laws, and the latter from abstaining from whatever defiles; 3d, Observance of festival days, which are numerous; 4th, Pilgrimages; and, 5th, The worship of Kami, both in the temples and in private dwellings. For pilgrimages there are twenty-two chief holy places, besides many smaller ones. Preëminent among them is the temple of Isye, in the island Nifon, which is to the Sintoos what Mecca is to the Mohammedans. One pilgrimage, at least, to this shrine is incumbent upon every one, and the very pious go annually. But the most remarkable feature in this religion is the doctrine of purity and pollution in regard to acts harmless or indifferent in themselves, in which respect it agrees with that of the Hindoos, and differs entirely from any form of belief among the Chinese. External purity is one of the most stringent parts of the Sintoo religion. This consists in abstaining from blood, from eating of flesh, and from communication with dead bodies. Those who have rendered themselves impure by any of these things are thereby disabled from going to the temples, from visiting the holy places, and in general from appearing in the presence of the gods. Whoever is stained with his own or any other blood, is impure for seven days. Whoever eats the flesh of any four-footed beast—with one or two exceptions—is impure for thirty days. Whoever eats the flesh of a fowl, wild or tame—water-fowl, pheasants, and cranes excepted—is impure only for a Japanese hour, which is two of ours. Whoever kills a beast, or is present at a public execution, or attends a dying person, or comes into a house where a dead body lies, is impure for that day. But of all other things which are impure, none are reckoned so very contagious as the death of parents and near relations. The nearer you are related to the dead person, so much the greater the impurity. All ceremonies which are to be observed on this occasion, the times of mourning and the like, are determined by rule. They have no idols in their temples: there are images of Kami, but, these, it is alleged, are not for purposes of worship. The only decorations in the older temples were a mirror, the emblem of purity of the soul, and some strips of white paper also, as emblems of purity. The festivals all begin with a visit to the temple. There the votary performs his ablutions at a reservoir provided for the purpose: he then kneels down in the veranda opposite to a grated window, through which he gazes at the mirror, and offers up his prayers, with a sacrifice of rice, fruit, tea, and the like. This done, he drops his coin in the money-box and retires. The money thus contributed is applied to the support of the priests of the temple.

The religion of Buddha—an off-shoot of Brahminism—is said to have been introduced to Japan A.D. 69, but to have made very little progress until the sixth century. It is now by far the most prevalent religion of the country, but is much mixed up with the ancient worship, and the ancient worship with it.

The philosophy of Confucius was early introduced into Japan, but is confined to the higher and more educated classes. It is rather a system of philosophy than a religion: it inculcates no particular faith and accommodates itself to any. It is compounded of most of the moral precepts of Confucius and some high mystic Buddhist notions. In some of its features it borders closely upon Pantheism. It has no religious rites and ceremonies of its own.

Of the two principal religions, it would appear that there are many sects. Liberty of conscience, so far as it does not interfere with the interests of the government, or affect the peace and tranquillity of the empire, has been at all times allowed. It was on political, and not on religious grounds that Christianity was driven out. A curious illustration of this toleration is given in an account of the shipwreck on the coast of Japan of the governor-general of the Philippines in 1608.

It was given upon his return to Spain, and is as follows: "There are no less than thirty-five different sects or religions in Japan. Some deny the immortality of the soul, others acknowledge divers gods, and others adore the elements. All are tolerated. The priests of all sects having concurred in a request to the emperor that he would expel our monks from Japan; the prince, troubled with their importunities, inquired how many different religions there were in Japan. Thirty-five was the reply. Well, said he, where thirty-five sects can be tolerated, we can easily bear with thirty-six: leave the strangers in peace." We have other testimony to the same effect in reference to toleration. Every citizen has a right to profess what faith he pleases, and to change it as often as he thinks fit. No one appears to care whether he does it from conviction or from regard to interest. Not only is any belief tolerated, but even the absence of all belief; in short, every mood of mind that does not vex the political mood of the empire. It frequently happens that the members of one family follow different sects, yet this difference of faith never occasions ill will or disputes. The making of proselytes, however, is prohibited by law.

Education, in so far as this consists in reading and writing, is universal even among the lowest ranks in Japan. There are colleges and academies throughout the empire in all the principal towns. There would seem also to be something like a national system of education, for the children of both sexes, and of all ranks, are invariably sent to rudimentary schools, where they are all taught to read and write, and are initiated into some knowledge of the history of their own country. There are immense numbers of cheap easy books continually issuing from the Japanese press, designed for the instruction of children and poor people. Books of a higher order are produced for the rich and better educated—reading being a favorite occupation with both sexes. Printing from blocks, after the Chinese fashion, was introduced in the beginning of the thirteenth century. Books are profusely illustrated with wood-cuts engraved on the same block with the type, and the Japanese are not ignorant of the art of printing in colors.

The Japanese carry on a large internal traffic, which from the peculiar characteristics of their country, is in a great measure by coasting. The numerous straits and creeks, with their shallow waters, though generally unfit for ships of burden, are sufficiently commodious for the small craft of the natives, which rarely exceed sixty tons. The inland transport is by horses, oxen, and porters, there being very little river or canal navigation. That the Japanese are a commercial people may be inferred from the order, neatness, and propriety with which everything connected with their trade is conducted. They have gold, silver, and copper money, as well as bills of exchange. Their shops have signs, and their goods are packed and labelled with a truly mercantile neatness. The foreign intercourse of Japan was more than two centuries, and till the date of our treaty, solely confined to the Dutch and Chinese. Even with these the trade was limited, being with the Dutch for a considerable time restricted to a single ship annually, and with the Chinese to ten junks. The exports and imports were even limited as to value, and the sales and purchases fixed by a tariff of the Japanese government. The Dutch were confined to the small island of Dezima, in the harbor of

Nagaski, which is only about 640 feet in length by 240 feet in extreme breadth. A small stone bridge connects the island with the town, and a strong Japanese guard was always stationed here, no one being allowed to pass either to or from the island without license. The whole island is surrounded with a high fence, on the top of which are placed iron spikes. On the north side are two water gates which were kept always shut, except to admit or let out the Dutch vessels. When a ship arrived her guns and ammunition were first taken out, and she was afterward searched in every part, and an exact list made of everything on board. The crew were then permitted to land on the island, where they were kept, as long as the ship remained, under the inspection of guards. Every Japanese official at the Dutch factory was bound twice or thrice a year to take a solemn oath of renunciation and hatred of the Christian religion, and was made to trample crosses and crucifixes under his feet. The Dutch were at all times surrounded with spies, whom they were obliged to employ as interpreters, clerks, servants, etc.

The commodities chiefly in demand in Japan are iron, steel, lead, tin, quicksilver, cinnabar, sapan wood, black pepper, cloves, nutmegs, sugar, putchuk, deer skins, ivory, Chinese and Tonquin raw silk, Indian cotton goods, cotton yarn, mirrors and other glass ware, and woollens. At one time or other all these articles have found a market in Japan. We may suppose that iron, steel and timber, high priced commodities there, will now become the staple articles of trade. In the earlier period of her intercourse, Japan was not only free to all the world, but trade was not even burdened with imposts on either ship or cargo; presents, however, had to be made to the emperor, the principal governors and a few others.

From the clause in Commodore Perry's treaty, entitling the ships and citizens of the United States to be received upon the same footing in Japan as those of the most favored nation, our privileges in that country steadily but silently advance, as other powers press upon the Japanese government and obtain treaties opening other ports and conferring other commercial advantages. It is true that the Dutch and Chinese retain a certain preference, which they have long enjoyed, and which was made a special exception to the clause above referred to; but in the natural course of events this exception must disappear, and the ports and trade of Japan be absolutely opened to the fleets and traffic of the world. We have over 700 whale-ships, manned by some 18,000 of our countrymen, employing a capital of more than $25,000,000, and yielding returns to those engaged in it of some $5,000,000 per annum. A very large proportion of these ships annually visit the seas in the neighborhood of the coasts of Japan, and the advantage of having convenient ports to refit and refresh in must prove very considerable indeed. Estimating the capacity of the people of that empire for the consumption of commodities of foreign production by those of other countries similarly situated —as we have already done the population and revenue—there will in all probability be an import trade carried on, by all nations, of about $10,000,000 per annum; and paid for in various trifling manufactured articles, but chiefly by the produce of the mines.

The many fruitless attempts made to open the ports of Japan, by various nations, unaccompanied by that display of physical force necessary to command due respect for their request; and the immediate success of Commodore Perry at the head of his formidable fleet, point significantly toward the kind of diplomacy best calculated to prove prosperous in that country, as in other parts of Asia. It appears not a little chimerical to expect any very beneficial result, to either the Japanese or ourselves, to spring from the presence of the present embassy. Indeed, we doubt much if the narrative of its adventures, by sea and land, will have more effect in enlightening the natives upon its return, and giving them any real insight into western ways and institutions, than had those of Marco Polo, or Sir John Mandeville, in advancing the knowledge of Europeans in regard to the nations of the East. Many things in America—that, in themselves, are so simple that any of our schoolboys could give an intelligible account of them—must prove not a little bewildering to the understanding of our Oriental guests. The journal of the sights and marvels seen in the United States by the Japanese Ambassadors—if ever it be translated into any European tongue—will be a great curiosity indeed, and perhaps surpass everything in the shape of travels that has appeared since the publication of those of the renowned Lemuel Gulliver.

THE END.

www.ingramcontent.com/pod-product-compliance
Lightning Source LLC
Chambersburg PA
CBHW031551110426
42739CB00039B/1048